The
Tiger
who was
Angry

Designer: Fiona Hajée

Consultant: Cecilia A. Essau, Professor
of Developmental Psychopathology,
at Roehampton University

First published in the UK in 2012 by
QED Publishing
A Quarto Group Company
230 City Road
London EC1V 2TT

www.qed-publishing.co.uk

A catalogue record for this book is available from the British Library.

ISBN 978 1 84835 848 5

Printed in China

The Tiger who was Angry

Rachel Elliot
John Bendall-Brunello

QED
QED Publishing

The animals were getting ready
for the Great Jungle Race.

The first to reach the Big Banyan
Tree would be the winner.

Only Tiger
was taking the
race seriously.

"I'm going to win!" said Tiger.
"I'm the fastest and the best."

The other animals agreed.
"You're bound to win," they said.

But Tiger wanted them to try to beat him!
"Don't you care about winning?" he shouted.

"It's just a bit of fun," said Tiger's best friend Rhino.

"No, it isn't," Tiger argued. "You should take it seriously like me."

"We don't all have to be the same,"
said Mongoose.
"You're all wrong!" shouted Tiger.
"You're being stupid!"

The other animals were upset.
Tiger had completely lost his temper.

"Friends are more important than the race," said Rhino.
"No they're not!" snapped Tiger.

Tiger couldn't stop being angry.
The other animals stayed away from him.

"Why won't anyone play with me?"
shouted Tiger. "It's not fair!"

He felt cross
and lonely.

Wise Elephant sat down beside Tiger.
"Different animals are good at
different things," he said.

"I have a long nose.
Some animals have
short noses.

You are a fast runner.
Some animals are slow runners.

It's **all right** to be **different**."

"My friends won't play with me," said Tiger.
"You scared them away," said Wise Elephant.
"When you lose your temper, you hurt yourself as well."

Tiger thought about his friends. He didn't feel angry any more. He just felt sad.

"I love being friends with Rhino," he said. "That's more important than winning."

Tiger and the other animals
lined up at the starting line.
"Ready, steady, GO!" said Wise Elephant.

WHOOSH!

Tiger set off in a blur of fur!
He was in first place, all by himself.

Rhino set off
quickly but was soon
plodding along slowly.

The other animals were running and laughing together.

Tiger stopped. He turned around
and ran back to his best friend.

"Come on, Rhino," he said with a grin. "Let's run together."
"But I'm not fast enough," said Rhino.

"Yes, you are," said Tiger.
"You're just right. You're
my best friend."

Rhino told lots of jokes, and
Tiger laughed and laughed.

Mongoose overtook them.

Even Pangolin overtook them.

But Tiger and Rhino didn't even notice.
They were too busy having fun!

Rhino and Tiger were the last to reach the Big Banyan Tree.

But they were both wearing the BIGGEST smiles.

"Three cheers for Rhino
and Tiger!" shouted
Wise Elephant.

"When I felt angry, I was all alone," Tiger said.
"It's much more fun being friendly!"

Next steps

- Look at the front cover of the book together. Ask your child to name all the animals in the book: tiger, elephant, rhino, mongoose, pangolin, ox and gibbon. Then ask them which is their favourite animal and why.

- Ask your child why Tiger lost his temper and why the other animals stayed away from him. Then ask your child how Tiger felt when this happened.

- Discuss how other people might react if we behave in an unfriendly or aggressive way towards them.

- Ask your child what they remember about the conversation between Wise Elephant and Tiger.

- If your child was to choose Rhino or Tiger as their best friend, which of the two would they choose and why?

- At the end of the story, ask your child to draw a picture of their favourite animals running together and discuss what types of feelings these animals might have while they are running and being friendly towards one another.

Dealing with anger

Emphasize to your child that:

- we should not brag about ourselves

- we should respect the fact that each one of us is different and that we all have strengths and weaknesses

- we should respect other people's wishes and not force other people to do what we want them to do

- people react to what we say and do to them: if we are friendly towards them, they will be friendly towards us

- friendly people have many good friends and they have fun playing with each other; aggressive people do not have many friends and they often feel lonely.